managing
our work

john w.
alexander

inter-varsity press
downers grove, illinois 60515

This is a training
document of Inter-Varsity
Christian Fellowship.

ISBN 0-87784-352-X

Library of Congress Catalog
Card Number 72-186572

Printed in the
United States of America

table of contents

acknowledgements

The ideas in this book bear the imprint of two categories of people on my life.

One group has earned my respect because of their dedicated lives as disciples of Jesus Christ: They have taken seriously their stewardship of the potentials the Lord gave them. Through a mature discipline of time and talent they have managed their work well and have inspired others by their precepts and examples, loving the Lord Jesus Christ with all their hearts, souls, minds and strength.

The other group has earned my respect through well-conceived and carefully presented principles of management. In seminars, courses, roundtables, books and films, the staff and consultants of the Presidents Association and American Management Association have taught me numerous lessons about the principles, science and art of management. Gratitude is owed particularly to Mr. Lawrence A. Appley, President of the Board of Directors of the American Management Association, and to Mr. J. P. Barger, President, Dynatech Corporation, Cambridge, Massachusetts.

It is a joy to know some individuals who are in both groups.

Specific acknowledgement goes to Prof. Gene A. Getz (who teaches the course in Christian Education at Dallas Theological Seminary) for his encouragement.

John W. Alexander
President
Inter-Varsity Christian Fellowship

1

managing our work

"I've simply got too much to do. There just isn't time enough. Can anybody help me?"

How many students, housewives, pastors, business men and women, teachers, and on and on find themselves feeling and expressing such complaints? It is a chronic complaint among countless busy people.

Is there any solution?

The answer is "yes." This book endeavors to present just such an answer. The ideas are cast primarily in terms of an Inter-Varsity Christian Fellowship (IVCF) staff member, but the principles apply to any busy worker no matter what his vocation, and with only slight modifications the specific suggestions can be easily adapted to almost anybody.

the challenge and frustration of a large task

An IVCF member may sometimes feel that he faces a task with more to be done than time in which to do it. But this is true of any worthwhile job. Indeed, every person who is physically and emotionally healthy needs such a challenge. Place a healthy person in a job with more time available than the task requires, and he soon becomes bored. We desire that IVCF people find in their jobs considerably more to be done than time in which to do it.

But, then, we face a potential pitfall. One of the most frustrating feelings in life is to awaken to a new day and face so many tasks that we are overwhelmed by their magnitude. We feel even worse when we face that sort of week or month or year. If we fail to plan properly—to set realistic goals and to abide by them—we may feel swamped, throw up our hands in frustration, collapse from nervous exhaustion, and be forced to take an extended leave of absence or even resign from the job.

The solution to frustration and chaos is to commit ourselves to Jesus Christ and then endeavor, under his Lordship, to manage our work effectively. Either we manage our work or the work manages us.

Paul writing to the early churches seems to have had just this sort of management principle in mind:

I planted, Apollos watered, but God gave the growth. (1 Cor. 3:6)

Each man should examine his own conduct for himself; then he can measure his achievement by comparing himself with himself and not with anyone else. For everyone has his own proper burden to bear. (Gal. 6:4-5, NEB)

In applying these Scriptures to Inter-Varsity's ministry, we say that God gives increase in terms of regeneration (by which the Spirit of the Lord Jesus Christ is planted within believers), in terms of growth of the believer toward maturity in Christ Jesus, in calling out people to missionary service and in other aspects of his work among men. These accomplishments are the work of the Holy Spirit. We cannot program them.

Yet, we are responsible to perform our assignments under

God—to manage our work, make plans, set goals and then work to achieve them (to plant, water and harvest)—on the campuses of our country. "For God is at work in you, both to will and to work for his good pleasure" (Phil. 2:13).

our commitment to the Lord

In getting our work done, it is not basically a matter of our doing God's work for him. God is the active agent. Primarily it is *his* working in and through us.

In one sense we are his *instruments.* Our initial step, therefore, is committing ourselves to his hands, placing ourselves joyfully at his disposal to be used by the Holy Spirit to the glory of our Lord Jesus Christ. "Do not yield your members to sin as instruments of wickedness, but yield yourselves to God as men who have been brought from death to life, and your members to God as instruments of righteousness" (Rom. 6:13).

In another sense we are *workers together with God.* "So we are ambassadors for Christ, God making his appeal through us. . . . Working together with him, then, we entreat you not to accept the grace of God in vain" (2 Cor. 5:20; 6:1).

Daily, deliberately, voluntarily, let us dedicate ourselves— mind, emotions, will and body—to the Lord for the Spirit's cleansing, filling and anointing. Unless he flows through and empowers IVCF, we will accomplish nothing of lasting value, no matter how well we manage our work. "Unless the Lord builds the house, those who build it labor in vain" (Ps. 127:1).

Over the years the literature of Inter-Varsity (*HIS* magazine and publications of IVP) has included thousands of pages of material written to help a person commit himself to Christ. The IVP catalog and the cumulative indices to *HIS* can guide any person who desires assistance in committing his total person to the Lord Jesus Christ and loving the Lord his God with all his heart, soul, mind and strength.

But in another sense we have human freedom, and it is necessary for the committed Christian to *work* at serving God. Organizing our tasks and planning our time is not "unspiritual"—it is part of "working together with him." Little has been written about this aspect of the Christian's life. We honor God best when we manage our lives and our work wisely.

management defined

Synonyms for *management* include: *stewardship, leadership, supervision, administration*. The Bible has a great deal to say about these phases of working together as one body. Much of the book of Nehemiah, for instance, is a case study in management principles.

And God has appointed in the church . . . helpers, administrators. . . . (1 Cor. 12:28)

The work is too exacting for you; you cannot handle it alone. . . . Now search for able men among all the people, men who revere and are honest, men who despise unfair profits, and appoint them leaders of thousands, of hundreds, of fifties and of tens. Let them regularly administer justice. . . . It will make it easier for you and they will share with you the responsibility. (Ex. 18:18-22, MLB)

Thus, management may be defined in various ways, but basically, management is the disciplining of our time and energy to be of maximum help to those for whom we are responsible, helping them to accomplish their work and to develop to their greatest potential in character, personality and contribution to society. It is the stewardship of time, talent and wealth. Its prime objective is the development of people, not the doing of things. Lawrence Appley (President's Association) has put it:

Management is guiding human and physical resources in dynamic organizational units which attain their objectives to the satisfaction of those served and with a high degree of morale and sense of attainment on the part of those performing the service.

Accordingly, management is a *ministry* to people, not a manipulation of them.

Tend the flock of God that is your charge, not by constraint but willingly, not for shameful gain but eagerly, not as domineering over those in your charge but being examples to the flock. . . . Likewise you that are younger be subject to the elders. Clothe yourselves, all of you, with humility toward one another. . . . (1 Pet. 5:2-5)

Preparing individuals and keeping them prepared for management requires effort, time and money. We cannot leave good management to grow like Topsy. The hit-or-miss, rule-of-thumb approach is inadequate. Management development is more effective when organized and planned. Moreover, it is an individual process. People in management must develop *themselves*; no one else can do it for them. On the other hand, this development can be helped when opportunity and assistance are made available. It is the duty of every leader to provide such opportunity and assistance for individuals under his direction. Let us assume that every one of us wants to do well. It is management's job to see that we are in situations and environments where we can do exactly that.

Management ability is one of the *gifts* of the Holy Spirit (1 Cor. 12:28). It is also a *science.* There is a body of knowledge and principles (acquired through the experience of our predecessors) to be learned. Further, management is an *art.* There are specific aptitudes and skills to be developed through sustained practice.

Management is a *profession* in its own right, a high calling. A good teacher does not necessarily make a good college president, nor a good preacher a good bishop, nor a good IVCF campus staff member a good area director. When a man is called up to manage and his only preparation is the knowledge and skill required in his former position, he faces a difficult adjustment. He needs to be trained in effective methods of management.

One of the most important principles in management is this: The person who makes the decision must bear the responsibility. We live in a day in which society clamors for the privilege of decision-making but manifests little willingness to shoulder the burden of responsibility for those decisions. A manager must pay a high price for the privilege of serving in a management position.

the making of a good manager

In Psalm 78:72 is this tribute to a good manager: "With upright heart he tended them, and guided them with skilful hand."

The basic reason for desiring to manage our work should be to be better stewards of the time, talent and wealth which God has given us. May the Lord Jesus make us the best leaders possible with the endowments we have received from him.

There are four elements of authority or power which a good manager possesses in varying degrees as he endeavors to influence his people.

The first is *position.* This authority is bestowed upon him by his supervisor.

The second element, *character,* must be cultivated. Its growth requires a long time, but it can be shattered overnight. Over the long haul, this is probably the strongest power of all.

The third element of the authority of a good manager, *personality,* is a gift. Some people have a forceful personality that other people respond to and trust in. Some do not have much of such potential. Those who have it can develop it.

Competence, the fourth power, is earned over a long period and is a result of both a record of deeds done and the spirit in which they are done.

A good manager will understand, however, that along with his authority comes a distance from his people. One of the prices a man is likely to pay in accepting a position of leadership is the weakening of some friendships with those who become his supervisees. A penalty for leadership is loneliness. Psychologists have discovered this strange force at work among groups of people functioning as teams and led by leaders. It is termed *positional distance,* which in advanced stages becomes *positional resistance.* The consequence of this force is to increase the feeling of distance; it may even go so far as to generate hostility between a person and his leader.

Examples are legion. From a group of campus staff members, one is promoted to area director. It won't be long until his former peers begin to feel farther from him. A man becomes president and finds himself "over" a man who was previously a close friend. It isn't long until the friendship tends to weaken; personal warmth may give way to cool formalism in the professional relationship. Positional distance and resistance can change the relationship between wives. It is possible that two couples who have been friends will drift apart if one of the men becomes the other's supervisor.

A good manager must understand this phenomenon, prepare for it and not hold it against his team.

the stewardship cycle of management

Managing our work as good stewards involves three major functions which we perform concurrently and repeatedly: planning, execution and review. *Planning* involves asking the questions: What should be done? Why? Where? Who should do it? How should it be done? *Execution* is carrying out the plans which result from answering those questions, and *review* comes during and after the action as we observe and evaluate. (See Figure I.) We will discuss each major function in depth in the three succeeding chapters.

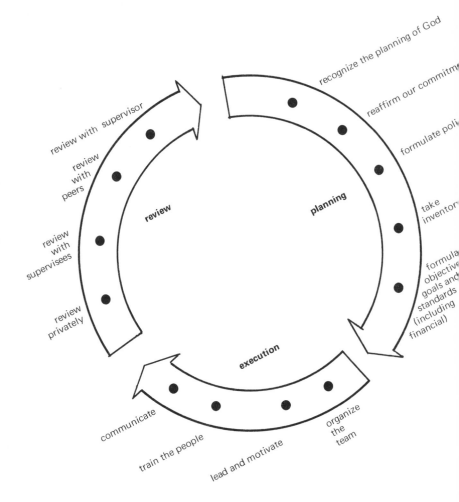

planning
- recognize the planning of God
- reaffirm our commitm[ent]
- formulate poli[cy]
- take inventor[y]
- formula[te] objective[s] goals and standards (including financial)

review
- review with supervisor
- review with peers
- review with supervisees
- review privately

execution
- organize the team
- lead and motivate
- train the people
- communicate

figure 1/the management cycle

2 planning

Planning is deciding in advance *what* should be done, *why* it should be done, *where* it should be done, *when* it should be done, *who* should do it and *how* it should be done (most of the decision of how is usually delegated to the person shouldering the responsibility).

five major steps in planning

There are five major steps in the planning stage of management:
1. Recognizing the planning of God. We believe the Scriptures teach that God is the great master planner who before the earth existed laid out a plan for all human history (Eph. 1:9-10). We believe his plan applies to both groups and individuals. Our earnest desire is that God will reveal his plan for IVCF in general and for every member in particular. We believe he desires to do this. We do not construct plans and take them to him for

endorsement; rather it is God who takes the initiative.

As I have planned so shall it be. (Is. 14:24)

For I know the plans I have for you, says the Lord, plans for welfare and not for evil, to give you a future and a hope. (Jer. 29:11)

Commit your work to the Lord, and your plans will be established. (Prov. 16:3)

2. Reaffirming our commitment. In IVCF we have three areas of commitment: the IVCF basis of faith, the purposes of IVCF and the IVCF policy manual.

IVCF has two sets of purposes: First, from the viewpoint of the *on-campus ministry* the purposes are to evangelize, disciple and promote missions. Second, from the viewpoint of the *incorporated movement* the purposes are to establish, train, assist and encourage groups of students and faculty who are committed to evangelism, discipleship and missions at colleges, universities, nursing schools and other tertiary schools in the United States.

3. Formulating policies. A policy is an answer worked out in advance to an anticipated question. It is a rule by which people abide as they work to fulfill their purposes. Such rules should be *in writing,* embodied in a policy manual which is available to everybody directly involved. The purpose of a policy manual is to provide a group of people with consistent answers to recurring questions. Well-conceived policies which are understood and followed by a group enable them to maximize their collaboration toward goals and minimize the amount of energy drained off by friction, uncertainty and confusion; good policies thus maximize the use of energy and time for making progress toward the fulfillment of the set purposes.

4. Taking inventory. First, we must take inventory of the *status of our work.* This may include a census which can serve to help us review our work, plan for the future and give an account to those who employ us. Second, there may be *external conditions* to which we must or should relate. Third, we must know the *resources* available to us: people (including our own time, energy and abilities), materials and financial resources.

5. Formulating objectives, goals and performance standards. In this context, the terms *purpose, objective, goal* and *performance standard* have distinct meanings:

A *purpose* is a broad statement of an aspiration. It describes the general direction in which we desire to go; for example, to win the conference football championship or to evangelize our school. IVCF's purposes are spelled out in the Articles of Incorporation as evangelism, discipleship and missions.

An *objective* is a more specific statement of an aspiration which, if attained, will produce progress toward fulfilling the purpose; for example, to win this particular football game or to conduct evangelistic discussions on our campus this year. In IVCF each person's objectives are spelled out in his job description (which is described more fully later in this chapter and also in chapter three). Or, looking at it in terms of problem solving, an objective is the solution to a problem.

A *goal* is a still more specific statement of what is to be accomplished to produce progress toward an objective; for example, to cross the goal line or to conduct evangelistic meetings in dormitories each semester. Or, to continue the problem-solving perspective, a goal is the adequate testing of a possible solution to a problem.

A *performance standard* is a measurement by which performance can be evaluated. Standards can be expressed in terms which are relative to a purpose or an objective or a goal; for example, to cross the goal line in harmony with the rules of the game or to conduct one evangelistic meeting per week in a dormitory.

These, then, are five steps involved in good planning. The first four are self-explanatory and probably more familiar than the fifth step. So we will now develop the fifth in more detail—exactly why and how we can formulate objectives, goals and performance standards so that we can plan effectively.

overcoming reluctance to plan specifically

Some Christians feel that our plans will deny the Holy Spirit freedom to act. This attitude, however, seems to ignore the primary factor involved in our planning—recognizing that God is the master planner. His plan was laid out before time began (1 Pet. 1:20; Eph. 1:9-12). The Holy Spirit is both a long-range and short-range planner. We limit him when we assume he operates only on spur-of-the-moment caprice. He has a plan for each life. He has a plan for each IVCF chapter and for the incorporated movement. It is our privilege to ask his guidance in setting objectives, goals and standards in harmony with his plan. It is poor stewardship of time and energy to commence a year, week or day without endeavoring to plan it as he directs. Once the specific plan is formulated, we execute it ever mindful that if he chooses to overrule, we are willing subjects to his divine prerogative.

A more practical reason a person may shy away from planning is that sculpturing statements of objectives, goals and standards is hard work. It is much easier to settle for vague generalizations of what we might undertake. Then, too, some people are lazy. They are afraid to agree to a job description and to adopt goals and standards which will disrupt their easygoing life style.

More basically, however, reluctance to plan specifically may reflect a person's insecurity. Once shared with other people, our objectives, goals and standards become criteria by which others can evaluate us. Human nature shies away from such exposure. It is easier to conceal our flaws if others have no measuring sticks we consider valid to appraise our performance. Thus, an insecure person is threatened by the demand of goals and standards and may tend to avoid them for fear his weaknesses or poor work may be thus revealed. But, a secure person welcomes goals and standards because he knows that his good work will thereby be unveiled; furthermore, he desires all the help available and realizes that goals can facilitate his receiving that help.

One also hears the statement that planning in general and goal-setting in particular stifle creativity. I challenge that proposition. It is true that poorly-conceived goals and poorly-constructed standards might thwart a person whose creativity moves by whim or one who is a loner and not able to work as a member of a team. But, well-conceived goals and standards stimulate and challenge a creative person who is able to direct his creative energy, especially when his colleagues depend on his productivity and he is willing to have his work evaluated.

I am convinced that creativity and discipline can go well together. Graham Blaine, Harvard University psychiatrist, says (in *Youth and the Hazard of Affluence* [New York: Harper and Row, 1966]) that creative people will produce more and be more free to produce if they have learned submission to authority—and self-discipline—early in life.

Within IVCF as a total family (students, faculty, staff, corporation, local committees and friends) is an enormous amount of creativity. Let us encourage and stimulate this potential in every possible way. Let us urge people to think creatively on every issue and problem, to be bold to experiment with new objectives, fresh strategies (the concepts which find expression in our objectives) and tactics (the things we do to reach our goals) and to innovate wherever desirable so that we can more effectively fulfill our purposes.

the importance of objectives, goals and performance standards

The foremost reason for having objectives and goals is to help get a particular job done. One IVCF area director expressed it: "In evangelism we have gotten into as many campuses this fall as we did the entire year last year. Much of this is attributable to goal-setting which was done as a team last summer."

Performance standards help get the job done properly while they also help a particular person improve himself. Standards identify areas which need improvement and can be key tools to develop more and more the potential of a person; they facilitate both self-appraisal and review of one's performance with another person.

The personal benefits which result from setting goals and standards are extremely important. First, they can help you appraise yourself, to appreciate and enjoy your work and to see ways in which you can do a better job. Second, they can reduce frustration and increase your satisfaction and sense of achievement. Third, they can help your colleagues help you do a better job. And fourth, they can provide *objective* rather that *subjective* criteria as bases for review of your work. This is why goals and standards should be expressed in writing. Written objective criteria should clarify the manner in which you are being evaluated by yourself, by your supervisor, by your supervisees and by your peers. All four parties have in front of them the same picture of what you are attempting to do and hopefully will use this same objective yardstick (your well-conceived and well-phrased standards) in reviewing your performance. And, if all goes well, they should arrive at the same answers to the questions: Which goals is this person hitting? Which is he missing? Which is he surpassing?

All of these benefits are reflected in the morale of an individual and group. There are at least three prerequisites for a high morale. These prerequisites parallel the benefits of goals and standards. First, a man must know his job description—What am I supposed to do? Then, he must know what results are expected—How well am I supposed to do the job? And finally he must know how well he is actually doing the job—Am I meeting the standards?

One of the most pleasant experiences in working together with a team occurs when a man knows he has done a good job, when his supervisors and supervisees know it and when he knows that they know it. Performance standards make this high morale possible. To be sure, our primary concern is that we please the Lord Jesus Christ and do a good job according to his standards; but we believe in the fellowship of believers and in the principle that evaluation by the brethren is one way by which the Holy Spirit communicates his counsel to us.

attributes of a good standard

We have been referring to *well-conceived* or *well-phrased* standards. What, exactly, makes a standard helpful? Standards represent before-the-fact agreement between supervisor and super-visee as to results which will be considered satisfactory. Whether or not the standards have been attained must be objectively observable and not subject to after-the-fact debate. Thus, a good standard describes the specific results desired.

Second, a good standard is worded to include accurate objective measurements rather than generalized subjective opinions. It answers such questions as: How much? By what time? How well? As compared with what? In collaboration with whom? At what cost?

Third, a good standard is worded to prevent misinterpretation. It is clear, not vague. Words to avoid include: *approximate, as soon as possible, maximum, minimum, few, satisfactory, desirable, justifiable, reasonable, effectively, adequately.* Such words can be useful in formulating goals, but they are not acceptable in formulating standards because there is going to be disagreement sooner or later as to whether or not the standard has been reached. If words such as these are used, the statement should be recognized as an expression of a goal rather than a standard.

constructing objectives, goals and standards
Goals and standards should be jointly constructed and realistically accepted by both the person and his supervisor. (Sometimes a man will set higher standards for himself than his leader would set for him.)

The first step in constructing objectives, goals and standards is to study the *job description* agreed upon by the person and his supervisor. The job description should provide the person with answers to three basic questions: For what am I responsible? To whom am I responsible? For whom am I responsible?

The second step is to express as an objective each entry in the job description. Then, one can construct specific goals for each objective. Finally, he can construct standards for each goal (or, if he so chooses, he can spell out standards directly in terms of objectives).

It bears repeated emphasis that standards should be made in

terms of results which are objectively observable. When this is impossible, they should be formulated in terms of actions to be carried out to increase the probability of good results. For example, we in IVCF cannot set standards in terms of number of conversions to Jesus Christ, but we can set standards in terms of our presentation of the gospel.

One of the most effective ways to construct a standard is to complete a sentence such as, "Satisfactory performance in respect to [the specified purpose or objective or goal] has been attained when...." Implicit in this statement should be the idea of "at least" rather than "at most," comparable to a floor, not a ceiling.

For example: If a secretary's job description carries an entry, "Is responsible for processing outbound letters from her supervisor," one of her standards might read, "...when she has ready for his signature every letter within twenty-four hours after she receives copy or dictation from him." If an IVCF staff member's job description contains an entry, "Calls on pastors in the interest of IVCF," one of his standards might read, "...when he calls on at least three pastors each month." In these examples the standards are spelled out directly in terms of objectives. This is a valid procedure, as mentioned before.

It is difficult enough to compose goals and standards dealing with quantity. It is more difficult to compose ones dealing with quality. And IVCF is a movement which emphasizes quality more than quantity. What kind of goals and standards, for example, should you compose dealing with evangelism? How do you know whether you are doing well or poorly in personal evangelism? in group evangelism? What standards can be set for effectively training others in evangelism? in discipling? Difficult though such quality standard-setting might be, let us do our best to compose statements that will help, knowing that even an imperfect statement is better than none.

A caution must be noted here. It is possible to overplan (to set too many goals or write them out in excessive detail) or to set standards too high. Both are errors. The result is a plan which frustrates the planner. Instead of a tool to help, it becomes a monster which enslaves and can generate a sense of guilt.

One staff member who had attempted too much wrote, "While staff service has been one of the most exciting and growth-producing experiences in my life, I leave it with a sense of defeat and guilt. The pressures upon one who is highly motivated (as are most IVCF staff members) are tremendous. These coupled with external pressures coming from many sources and in subtle ways can cripple a personality." Other staff have used expressions such as "frustrated at not being able to do as much as I would like," "overwhelmed by lack of time," "badly overworked, frustrated at not doing enough," "under immense pressure," "so involved with so many people in so many places that I am helping no one and am carrying a load of guilt."

The solution is not to abandon goals and standards. We must avoid the extreme of underplanning as well as overplanning. A person who finds through experience that his endeavors are overplanned or that his goals are too ambitious can rectify the plan by scaling down the standards to workable size.

Figure 2 gives one example of the relationship of purposes to well-constructed, realistic, qualitative objectives, goals and standards.

the role of leadership in goal- and standard-setting
Occasionally it is said that a leader must choose between being "people-centered" and "goal-centered," the implication being that the two are mutually exclusive. Our philosophy of goal-setting is based on the premise that the two are *not* in contradiction and that a leader who loves people and is a good manager can be both people- and goal-centered.

Every leader should have two sets of objectives, goals and standards: one for *himself* as a person and one for the *team* which he leads (e.g., his local chapter, cell group, area team, department team). See Figure 3.

These two sets of objectives, goals and standards should be further differentiated by time: an annual and a long-range plan. The annual plan spells out objectives, goals and standards which

figure 2/purposes, goals, objectives, standards

purposes

Purposes should be the same for all members of the team. As homogeneous elements, the purposes unify the organization.

objectives

Objectives vary from person to person depending on their positions. Job descriptions should be spelled out in such a way that each entry is, in itself, an objective to be achieved. In different words, a man's objectives are the responsibilities which he has shouldered. There usually are two or more objectives for each purpose.

example A

One of the purposes of IVCF is to train, assist and encourage groups of students and faculty who are committed to evangelism, discipleship and missions.

examples under A

1. To provide a field staff of qualified men and women to train IVCF local chapters.
2. To publish a periodical designed primarily for college students and faculty.

example B

One of the purposes of a local IVCF chapter is to evangelize the campus.

examples under B

1. To help Christian students understand what the Bible teaches concerning evangelism.
2. To train Christian students in proclaiming the gospel and in persuading their peers.

goals

Goals are specific statements of steps to be taken if the responsibility is to be discharged and the objective is to be achieved. There usually are two or more goals for each objective.

standards

Standards are specific statements of conditions to be met if the goal is to be reached. There usually are two or more standards for each goal.

examples under A-1

a. To maintain a procedure for recruiting high quality new staff prospects.
b. To maintain a procedure for training both new and veteran staff members to fulfill their task of training local chapters.

examples under A-1-b

i. A period of orientation for new staff is conducted once a year.
ii. Each area director conducts a training conference for his staff team at least once a semester.

examples under B-2

a. To have each Christian student involved in personal evangelism on a regular basis.
b. Staff members to take students "fishing" in order to demonstrate how to engage in personal evangelism.

examples under B-2-a

i. When each Christian student is in one evangelistic conversation per week and gives the peer a call to commitment to Jesus Christ.
ii. If the peer refuses to commit himself, the Christian understands the point at which the peer is rejecting the gospel.

we expect to reach "this year." A long-range plan (as we use the term in IVCF) expresses goals and standards which we aspire to achieve in the more distant future, beyond this year. The long-range plan gives continuity to our annual plans.

Within an organization, construction of goals and standards should begin at the top. Let the chief executive first construct his own goals and standards and circulate copies throughout the movement so that any person who desires to study them has opportunity to do so. A person is more likely to participate if he sees his supervisor working according to goals and standards.

An IVCF staff member, after completing his first set of goals, wrote his area director, "I cannot say I'm sorry to have them finished, but I certainly am glad that God changed my attitude about it all. Will you be sure to pass on to [the president] how much his own goals helped me understand for the first time just what goals are. Thanks."

If your supervisees have no such standards, begin by explaining yours. Let them suggest changes and additions. Then encourage your supervisees to sculpture their own goals and stan-

figure 3/personal and team objectives, goals and standards (ogs)

planning expresses itself in terms of:

position	personal objectives goals and standards	team objectives goals and standards
cabinet member	ogs for cabinet member	ogs for his team
area director	ogs for area director	ogs for his area
chapter president	ogs for chapter president	ogs for his chapter
leader of cell group	ogs for cell leader	ogs for his cell group
pastor	ogs for the pastor	ogs for his church
sunday school teacher	ogs for the teacher	ogs for his class

dards. Some will jump at the chance; others will hold back. Treat each man independently.

Most of our supervisees want the help available through well-constructed objectives, goals and standards. They recognize them as valuable tools for better service. Often, however, people have not had enough experience in such tool-making to produce their own. They need our help and most of them want it. If for some reason they do not come to us, we owe it to them to take the initiative in helping them construct these tools. On the other hand, there are some who are threatened by this tool-making; in such cases it will be an emotional struggle to help them succeed in using objectives, goals and standards.

If ignorance is the stumbling block, we must sit down with a supervisee and show him how to construct these tools (see chapter five, "How to Proceed"). If he is unable to construct a simple initial draft of his objectives, goals and standards, then we should construct a rough-draft copy for him to amend.

When a supervisee fails to produce a copy of these tools, he may be so overloaded that he cannot find time to plan his work or he may be undisciplined or it may even be that he does not respect you as a worthy recipient of such efforts on his part. Whatever the reason for his failure, it is our responsibility as supervisors to *set a deadline* by which he is to give us either an original rough draft or his amended copy of our draft. If a supervisor fails to do this, the morale of the team under that man may disintegrate in chaos and confusion.

If we have leadership responsibilities in any movement or organization, we are guilty of negligence if we permit any supervisee to operate without a written job description, if we do not possess a written copy of his objectives and goals, mutually acceptable to both and if we do not possess a written copy of the mutually agreeable standards. And we are more amiss if we accept new people on the team who are not willing to construct and use goals and standards.

Admittedly there are some types of positions where objectives, goals and standards are unnecessary—where the tasks are simple, repetitive, performed in close proximity to the supervisor and spelled out so clearly in the job description that goals or standards would not clarify anything. However, under most conditions a person would do well to produce the kind of plan discussed herein.

practical considerations for leaders

Leaders of movements which are required to operate in the black discover sooner or later that lack of money means that some positions go unfilled, some qualified people cannot be appointed and some duties cannot be delegated since no delegates are available. This means that some of our objectives, goals and standards must be set in terms of money to be procured and in terms of controlling the expenditure of money which comes in.

A *budget* is a tool by which management expresses its plans for handling money. It is a quantitative statement in terms of dollars (or other monetary unit) required to execute the plans. A manager should have a voice in constructing his budget; he should understand it and abide by it. A budget is not an end in itself, but a means to an end, an instrument to help us fulfill our purposes.

Expense controls are procedures for abiding by budgets. Statements pertaining to budgets and expense controls should be *in writing* with copies available to everyone who is directly involved.

the actual practice of planning

We have been saying that planning in general and goal-setting in particular are good in theory and useful in practice. People who are still skeptical about the whole process, however, will need to actually experience the benefits of setting and realizing goals before they become convinced of the importance of planning.

The following excerpts from a letter by a former IVCF staff member are pertinent: "This week I went to the Management Seminar co-sponsored by Far Eastern Gospel Crusade and Covenant Seminary. The Seminary provided the location and food and FEGC sent their home secretary, Olan Hendrix, to teach us.

"Now I understand why IVCF needs a long-range plan. I have carefully read the proposal for a Long Range Plan since the seminar without the blinders I previously had. I guess you would call my previous attitude towards management 'super-spiritual.' Now I can see with a bit more clarity how this can help both me and IVCF. I don't think I can put the things I learned in order of importance but I do want to share some of these exciting things with you.

"Certainly high on the list was that I saw that I need to be accountable to a human being, not just to God. This is something that even a Presbyterian seminary just didn't teach me. Olan pointed out that people want to be held accountable as long as it is not sprung on them. This idea ties in closely with a job description which the person already has. This not only helped me in my relationship upward to you, but it certainly has implications for what I am expecting from chapter presidents. Now that I have read the Proposal, I see that those thoughts aren't new to IVCF, but they certainly are to me. . . .

"Another major point was the emphasis on planning objectives and goal-setting.

"For some time I have realized that I needed to be thinking in a goal-directed way, but it has been the hardest job I have ever had. As Olan said, 'We prefer to do things rather than to think about them.' Unfortunately that is I all over. It makes for real dissatisfaction when I begin to evaluate what I have accomplished for our Lord. Maybe this is one reason why I have in the past liked to be involved in public speaking rather than administration. If by God's grace I can conquer my problem of lack of concrete achievable goals, I think this would change my life. Would you pray with me about this?"

Another letter from an IVCF staff member sheds further light: "I want to take this opportunity to tell you how much *Managing Our Work* has affected my personal life. At first I thought it unnecessary to write such detailed goals and standards, but now I can see how needed changes in my own life as well as direction in staff work have become a reality. The standards for measuring myself are no longer burdensome; they are incentives to achieve new challenges."

recapitulation

Effective planning within a team is a two-way street, a recipro-cating flow. Some planning moves from the top down (i.e., the chief executive should take initiative in leading the team in some of the planning), but some planning should move from the bottom up (the "bottom" being the lowest level of the organi-zation affected by the planning).

Accordingly every IVCF person is expected to become famil-iar with IVCF plans which affect him and then take the initia-tive in offering suggestions to his supervisor for improving them.

Plans can be expressed in many ways, but the method stressed here is to spell them out in terms of objectives, goals and standards. In this way we provide useful tools for budgeting and expending our energy and hours. This gives structure to our days, weeks, months and years. And, if properly constructed, these tools will be invaluable aids in preventing frustration and giving direction to our efforts.

Well-set objectives, goals and standards can also facilitate a sense of achievement which thrills a person who sees for himself that he is doing those things he knows he should be doing.

3   execution

Execution is carrying out the plans we have made—doing what we sense God wants us to do. This includes finding people to help with the work—organizing them as a team, motivating those we lead, training them for the task and communicating effectively with all who should be informed. Mr. Charles Foreman, vice-president of United Parcel Service, has put it well: *A good team is a group of capable people put together by design working with shared concern toward meaningful objectives according to a plan at high levels of performance within a framework of policies to which all are committed.*

four major steps in execution
There are four major steps in the execution stage of management:

1. Organizing the team. Organizing is dividing up all the activities and material and assigning them to people for purpose fulfillment. There may be a period, perhaps when a movement is young, in which its members can move within the last verse of the book of Judges, "... every man did what was right in his own eyes." But, if a movement remains in this unorganized state, it is likely to fragment into splinter groups. A team of people desiring to complement each other needs an optimal amount of structure, of organization. As a well-organized team, they can do more than the sum of their individual efforts.

2. Leading and motivating the team. It is not enough for a leader to construct his plans and organize the team. He must lead and motivate his people. Books have been written on each of these two themes, but the main point is to bring the plans off the drawing boards and into action, to transform the theory into deeds done.

3. Training the people. Training is systematic instruction. Its purpose is to help people fulfill the responsibilities listed in the description of their duties. In IVCF this means that we desire to train persons to be more Christlike in character and to do those deeds which will glorify Christ in their lives in general and as IVCF members in particular.

4. Communicating. Communication is the process by which a person makes his thoughts, hopes, desires, questions, knowledge and plans known to another person. Its objectives are to inform, persuade, consult, recognize, appreciate and participate. Good communication within an organized team is essential for general understanding of what is going on and for setting a climate for high morale. A well-managed team has wide-open communication channels so that the first sign of low morale anywhere in the movement can be spotted and remedial measures taken immediately.

These four major steps in execution occur at both the individual and the team levels. Since they are so essential, let us examine them in more detail.

overcoming reluctance to organize

Christian organizations face a peculiar problem. It pertains to the prevailing confusion between our attitude toward the sovereignty of God and our attitude toward organizing the work.

The issue involving God's sovereignty can be described as follows: "For all Christian activity the reality of the supernatural is the ultimate great divide. On one side, there are those who, in spite of what they say and write, have their essential confidence in rationalistic humanism; on the other side there are those who, in spite of some inconsistency, have their ultimate reliance upon the living God of the unseen world of the Spirit, the God who has revealed himself once and for all in his incarnate Son and in the Scriptures. True faith in the living God and true dependence upon him is this ultimate great divide." (C. Stacey Woods in *IFES Journal*)

The issue involving organization is whether we will plan our work, execute the plans and honestly evaluate the results (i.e., give an account). Again there is a great divide which separates the organized from the disorganized, the disciplined from the undisciplined, the planners from men of caprice, the evaluators from those who shun evaluation whether by themselves or others.

Confusion develops if we assume that these two great divides are synonymous. If we make such a mistake, the common conclusion is this: People who organize are unspiritual rationalistic humanists; people who leave things to the Holy Spirit are spiritual and to be emulated.

We tend to criticize "unspiritual organizers" because we suppose their basic confidence is in technique, in human persuasiveness, in man himself. Even if they seem to espouse a conservative theology, they are written off as people who have only an aura of spirituality and imagined divine approval. Either extreme—either the "power of God" seen as operating only when man eschews planning and organization or the "wisdom of man" operating through planned, well-organized endeavor independent of God—is incomplete and dangerous. Instead of superimposing the two great divides, let us intersect them at ninety degree angles. We then have four options rather than two.

Figure 4 shows how God the Holy Spirit can work in both well- and poorly-organized situations. The effort to organize does not necessarily force him out. We can also see that poor organization of a Christian movement is no guarantee that the Holy Spirit will work. The presence of the living God in a movement is related to the condition of the hearts of its members, not primarily to the degree or type of organization. Let us choose option two, thereby being on the right side of the vertical great divide and on the upper side of the horizontal great divide.

the importance of organization

One of the main causes for trouble in Christian organizations is the failure of members to know exactly who is responsible for what and who is responsible to whom. In this situation friction is certain to result sooner or later. It can be a serious mistake to assume that in any group "everyone already knows who is supposed to do what." Usually either a few men end up extremely overloaded or little is really accomplished well.

How many pastors and congregations are frustrated because there is no clear statement in writing on which both are agreed as to what the congregation can anticipate from the pastor and

figure 4/organization and reliance on God

	from the perspective of ultimate authority:	
	reliance on man	reliance on God
good organization	1	2
poor organization	3	4

from the perspective of managing our time and effort:

what the pastor can look for from the congregation? How many pastors have been raked over the coals by disgruntled laymen—when neither possessed written job descriptions spelling out what each could expect of the other? How many youth directors, choir directors, assistant pastors, special workers and people employed by non- or interdenominational movements have been hired with no written understanding of their specific responsibilities—and have subsequently been crushed?

How many thousands of man-hours have been wasted at board meetings—meetings of trustees, directors, elders, deacons, superintendents, teachers or any advisory board—because nobody had a clear enough concept of what the board was supposed to do and of what the individual board members were supposed to be doing? A board chairman is defaulting on a trust if he lets time go by without the production of both a job description for the board as a corporate body and a job description for each individual board member.

elements of good organization

Organization must include, first of all, *a good system of delegation.* Leaders must entrust to other persons the responsibility and performance of specified work with commensurate authority and with a mutual understanding of the expected results. The work load should be delegated to individuals, not to groups, not even co-directors.

Scripture gives an example of delegation in Exodus 18:18-23:

You are wearing out yourself and the people as well. The work is too exacting for you; you cannot handle it alone. Now listen to me; I have counsel for you, and God be with you. You represent the people before God and bring the cases to God. You make clear to them the rules and the laws; you show them the way to behave and what they ought to do. Now search for able men among all the people, men who revere God and are honest, men who despise unfair profits, and appoint them leaders of thousands, of hundreds, of fifties and of tens. Let them regularly administer justice for the people and only when

*there is an extremely difficult case, let them bring it to you; but
for ordinary affairs let them judge. It will make it easier for you
and they will share with you the responsibility. If you work this
out, and if God commands you, you will be able to stand the
strain and all these people will go home satisfied. (MLB)*

There are three components of good delegation: *responsibility* (identification of the duties to be performed), *authority*
(commensurate power to perform those duties) and *accountability* (requirement that the subordinate render a proper
account and report of what he has done with his delegated
responsibility and authority). A subordinate who fails to report
properly, who provides unsatisfactory accounts, is unworthy of
the trust delegated to him.

In deciding what to delegate and to whom it should be delegated, a leader does well to keep in mind two principles: First,
he must push responsibility (and commensurate authority) as
far "down" the management pyramid as possible. Second, it is
the leader's task to decide which decisions should be made by
what members of the team and when they should make them—
and then to see that they are made by the right people at the
right time. When this principle is followed, even a large team
can react swiftly and wisely to change.

Second, effective organization must involve the *definition of
relationships.* A leader must spell out clearly—in writing so all
can see—the relationships between team members. To do this,
he uses two essential expressions: job descriptions and organization charts.

Job descriptions should spell out clearly, in writing, the
answers to three basic questions for each person to whom responsibility and authority are delegated: To whom is he responsible? For whom is he responsible? For what is he responsible?
"According to the commandment of the Lord through Moses
they were appointed, each to his task of serving or carrying"
(Num. 4:49). Appendices A, B and C are examples of three
kinds of job descriptions for a board, a board member and a
chief executive officer.

Organization charts are diagrams which show each position in the organization and portray graphically the answers to the three questions addressed in the job descriptions. It is designed to picture lines of official relationship, not levels or status of positions. *Line* is a term which applies to the official relationship between a person and his supervisor; it is always a two-way street—a route along which official responsibility, authority and supervision flow in one direction and along which reports, recommendations and feedback flow in the opposite direction.

For example, within the IVCF staff is a line between a campus staff member and his area director, a line between an area director and his regional director and another line which connects a regional director with the president. Thus, the line ultimately links the chief executive with every person on the IVCF staff.

Producing an organization chart can be difficult, as can displaying it. If no such chart has been on public display in your domain, you may encounter resistance (either verbal or nonverbal), sometimes manifesting itself by comments such as "Why rock the boat?" or "Better let sleeping dogs lie." The fact that an organization chart is not welcomed may be prima facie evidence that something is wrong with the manner in which you are managing your team. To decide not to post it is taking the easy way out; it is no solution to the problem and it only postpones the day of reckoning.

Third, organization involves *selection of the right people.* A leader must recruit and screen people necessary to carry out the plans and then assign them to their positions in the organization. Each person is entitled to see in advance a clear statement of his job description and his place on the organization chart.

Whenever there is any kind of change in the assignment of people to positions, it is wise to call together everyone directly involved (that is, those whose positions are being changed plus their immediate supervisees) and explain who is changing positions and why. If the change is of general interest, announce it in the house organ. If only a few people are involved, tack up an announcement on their common bulletin board.

Fourth, good organization must include *selection of the facilities and materials.* In this area, two basic questions require answers: What building and capital facilities do our people need? What operating materials should they have available?

Finally, organization requires *money.* Three major functions must be carried out: procuring the money (receiving the income), controlling expenditures and keeping an account of both the inflow and outflow.

the basis for motivation

Once a leader has constructed his plans and organized his team, he must lead and motivate that team to get the job done well. This is the second major step in the execution stage of management.

However, a leader should not be expected to drum up motivation in a vacuum. Motivation needs a certain atmosphere to grow in. That atmosphere, that basis on which a leader can build, is *loyalty.*

If IVCF is to be strong, loyalty—first to Jesus Christ and then to one another—must be woven throughout its fabric. Each team member must have trust and confidence in the movement's basis of faith, its purposes and policies, his own ability and resources as used by the Holy Spirit to get the job done and his leaders all the way through the governing body.

In IVCF this means that a campus staff member must trust his area director, his regional director, his president and the IVCF board—and vice versa. An area director must similarly be loyal to his regional director, president and board, a cabinet member to the president and board—and vice versa. If such confidence pervades the movement, every member will feel a part of the whole team, as illustrated in Figure 5.

Loyalty is an important ingredient of fellowship. People enjoying genuine fellowship are a group loyal to one another and are motivated by one another. Any threat to their loyalty is a threat to their fellowship, to their motivation.

How, then, shall we proceed in situations where loyalty is threatened? The answer depends on where the threat occurs.

figure 5/pyramids of loyalty

from the perspective of fieldwork:

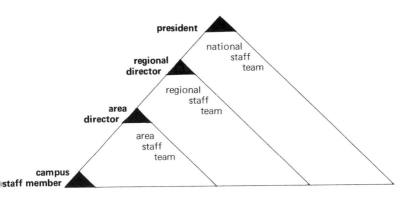

from the perspective of departmental alignment:

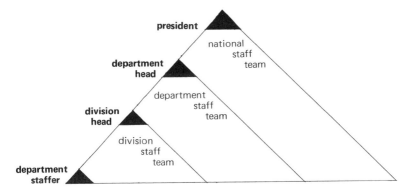

If the threat lies between two peers or between two men proximal "in the line," the problem should be worked out between the two men. Every written report should provide opportunity for a man to indicate any wavering in his loyalty to his supervisor. A disloyal man defaults on a trust if in such a written report he fails to level with his supervisor. Conversely, every response to such a report should convey an indication of the supervisor's awareness of the problem and willingness to level with the supervisee. If written communication is too stiff for airing the problem, surely review conferences (see chapter four) should expose it.

If the threat lies between two men who are "in the line" but not proximal, the initial responsibility for proceeding rests upon the intermediate supervisor. For example, if the president finds a department head who is not loyal to the board and its chairman, the president does not suggest that the chairman make a special trip to the department head in an effort to resolve the problem. This would be an abdication of one of the president's major duties which is developing within his supervisees loyalty to the board.

Likewise, if an area director learns that a campus staff member is having trouble maintaining trust and confidence in the president, the area director does not proceed to suggest that the president go to the staff member. The area director himself is failing in one of his foremost responsibilities—building within his team loyalty to the president.

After identifying the area of the threat to loyalty, how should an intermediate supervisor proceed? (It should be obvious that he himself must be loyal; otherwise he is hardly qualified to calm a restive team.)

First of all, let the intermediate supervisor research the symptoms of the disloyalty. Do his people lack information? People can hardly be loyal to a person about whom they have little or no knowledge. Or, are his people dissatisfied because they have been fed half-truths or false rumors? Are his people criticizing a person because they feel he is serving inadequately? A leader must earn the loyalty of his people. They are entitled to someone worthy of their confidence and commitment. Or, finally, is the problem due to strong differences of opinion? Loyalty can survive some differences of opinion, but there come times when a man differs so sharply with another that, although friendship may continue, loyalty as co-laborers in the same organization is strained beyond the breaking point.

Second, let the intermediary research the reasons the disloyal individuals feel as they do. If lack of information is the factor, why isn't adequate information getting through? If false witness is the cause, why is the grapevine poisoned? If the problem is inadequate service of a leader, the intermediary should analyze the weaknesses of the criticized person. If there are strong differences of opinion, the supervisor's job is to spell out clearly what he sees as the specific points of contention.

Third, the intermediate supervisor must now do all he can to rebuild and strengthen team loyalty to the person in question. He must fill the information vacuum and try to facilitate interaction between his people. He must quell false rumors and find out if somewhere in the picture there is a jealous individual who needs to be dealt with for sowing discord among his brothers (Prov. 6:16-19). He must help a leader overcome his flaws and also help his team see the person's strengths. He must try to keep two horses in the same harness from pulling in opposite directions. No small order.

Suppose the intermediate fails in these efforts. Then what? Let him ask his supervisor for help—and let them together, supporting each other, go to the unhappy people and repeat the procedures. If their team effort fails, they should take the problem farther up through proper channels.

If all these efforts are fruitless, one or all of the disgruntled individuals must leave the organization. Disloyalty poisons a movement. "A house divided against itself cannot stand."

elements of good motivation

Given the basic attitude of loyalty in his people, a leader can go on to fulfill his special responsibility to motivate the team. There are at least three major ways he can do so. The first is by *precept and example.* May our precepts be sound and may our example be that of mature people in whom Christ dwells, who love him with their total person. May we love Scripture, saturate our minds with it and moment by moment walk in its light. May we be men and women of prayer, practiced in praising God for his character and deeds, in thanking him for blessings given, in adoring him, in confessing sin and in interceding for others and petitioning him for ourselves.

The second way is *encouragement.* Those whom we lead are soldiers in vigorous warfare. At times they will need balm on their wounds and rest from the fray. When discouragement shatters their spirits, may we be ready with words of encouragement to lift their sagging souls.

The third motivating factor is *appreciation.* A person who never hears a word of commendation from his supervisor—or supervisees—may soon seek employment elsewhere. There is satisfaction in a job well done, but sometimes that is hard to measure, and approval from the person in charge is needed before the worker is convinced he has made a valuable contribution. Most people want to please their supervisor. When the supervisor recognizes the value of a person both as an individual and as a team member and when he commends a person's work as an important part of the whole operation, then one's work becomes easier and more rewarding. It is hard to do a thankless job carefully. One secretary comments, "At the end of a dictabelt he mailed in my boss said, 'Thanks very much for doing these letters, Mary. I don't know how I'd get along without you, even though I don't say it very often.' Well, I've been typing faster for three weeks on the strength of that word of praise. He hadn't said a thank you for months." Never forget that those working under you are *people*—and if even God desires praise, certainly we human beings need it.

elements of good training
Training, the third major step in execution, is systematic instruction. Its purpose is to help people fulfill the responsibilities listed in their job descriptions. It involves five fundamental

ministries: to *teach* people what their predecessors have learned so they will not have to learn everything the hard way, to *demonstrate* how to be and how to do what is expected of them, to *observe* them being and doing as they observe their trainer, to *evaluate* together and to *encourage* one another.

Carrying out those ministries calls for a training program which provides for production of training materials and aids, individual on-the-job training, group training at conferences and camps and development of ideas, concepts and skills.

Our training program is designed to help people work effectively and develop their potential as full-orbed persons, maturing disciples of Jesus Christ. (In this connection, you may wish to study a copy of *Training in IVCF*, available from the IVCF national office.)

Each IVCF member is expected to be thoroughly familiar with our training materials and to teach them diligently to those he leads.

the importance of communication

Good communication is essential to set a climate for high morale. In one sense communication is the medium through which leadership gets its job done. It is comparable to the environment. When the environment is foggy for lack of communication, misunderstanding flourishes, producing friction, inefficiency and many other troubles. When a leader has created a climate in which people enjoy working (regardless of their particular tasks), he has achieved a rich quality of management, a superior type of leadership. He has rendered a valuable service.

When disgruntlement starts to fester within an organization, poor communication is invariably one—if not the major—explanation. Some people may not have a clear picture of their job descriptions either before or after they are hired. Employees may receive a message different from the one a supervisor thought he gave as to what is expected in managing the job (deadlines, reports, etc.). Or, if those pictures were clear before employment, subsequent communication with supervisors, peers or supervisees may be inadequate.

Without good communication, a manager may even be unaware that problems exist. For example, when communication channels are open, a person who resigns will give a clear and accurate statement of his reasons to his supervisor. But when channels are clogged, he may tell his supervisor that his reason for resigning is that the organization stifles creativity, but tell a third party that he honestly felt he wasn't getting adequate supervision. Thus, low morale is generated and spread while the leader thinks everything is fine. The disgruntlement can spread irretrievably unless the boil is lanced—through good communication and corrective steps. A well-managed team must maintain wide-open communication channels so that the first sign of low morale anywhere in the movement can be spotted.

When a leader learns of a morale problem, he is wise to investigate the extent immediately. Is the restive person the only one who is unhappy? If not, who else is unhappy? If a campus staff member is restive, is his entire team unhappy? If the entire team is unhappy, are all the area teams uneasy?

elements of good communication

Communication is the process by which a person makes his thoughts, hopes, desires, questions, knowledge and plans known to another person. Its objectives are to inform, persuade, consult, recognize, appreciate and participate. It is both a science and an art.

To communicate effectively, a person must have a clear mental picture of what he wants to communicate; he must *formulate the content accurately.* This is the objective, scientific, verbal part of communication. It is *what* you say. But, for the communication to be complete, the person must also transfer that clear image to the minds of others. It is in this transference that communication is an art—a subjective, emotional, nonverbal artistic skill. It is *how* you say it.

Two broad types of skill are required. One-way communication involves the skill of getting others to understand us. Two-way communication involves our skill in helping others to make themselves understood by us.

Specialists say that seventy-five percent of all direct communication between individuals in personal contact is non-verbal. It is the tone of voice, the facial expression, the gesture, the whole silent language that envelops the words. (See Edward T. Hale, *The Silent Language* [New York: Fawcett, 1962].)

Man may preach the importance of facts, but he often makes judgments on the basis of the silent language he receives. To communicate effectively, therefore, a person must penetrate his own and his listener's rational facade and discover the true feelings involved. In this connection, a leader should ask himself two important questions: How well do I know myself—what kind of non-verbal messages am I sending out? How well do I know how my people react to me—what kind of non-verbal messages do they seem to be receiving and sending back to me?

Lawrence Appley has commented on our responsibility to help the receiving person respond most effectively to our communication: "Man is a sensitive creature, and some things cause him to tighten up to the point that he cannot react comfortably to some situations. . . . Those of us who are in positions of leadership and are responsible for developing and maintaining good human relationships should be extremely sensitive to what causes tenseness on the part of another person. When you pick up the telephone, or pick up a pen, or meet a person face to face, give consideration to the impact of what you say, or do, or write, upon the tenseness on the part of another person. What kind of climate do you create? When one of your people picks up the telephone and hears your voice, what is his immediate reaction before you have said anything other than the initial greeting? When he receives a letter or a memorandum from you, is he afraid to open it? When he gets a message from your secretary to come into your office, is he relaxed or in a mental state of concern that leads to tension? A manager, a leader responsible for the efforts of other people, must be continually careful of the way in which he approaches people so as to keep tension at a minimum."[1]

[1]Reprinted by permission of the publisher from *Management News*, January 1966. © 1966 by the American Management Association, Inc.

Thus, effective communication necessitates conveying our message in *a spirit which reflects a healthy attitude* toward ourselves and our listeners.

Another essential element of good communication is *leveling*. Leveling is being honest in communication. It consists of two basic ingredients: giving honest answers to questions which a person asks (non-verbally as well as verbally) and letting a person know exactly what we think and how we feel. This is a rare skill. Most of us either level too much by letting our tongues run wild in an unloving spirit or level too little by taking the easy way out and avoiding confrontations to which the other person is entitled. To harbor dissatisfaction is damaging for both him and us. Wisdom and love call for leveling. The hardest but most useful way is face-to-face confrontation; easier but less satisfactory is expressing our honest feelings in writing.

Helping supervisees to level with their supervisors—and vice versa—is hard work. I remember a field trip in which I spent a day with one of our field leaders, discussed many aspects of the work and finished by taking him and his wife out to dinner. I left town thinking that everything was moving along satisfactorily. A few days later I received a long letter in which the field leader itemized numerous complaints about the way I was leading IVCF, and he closed the letter by resigning. Obviously there was something wrong with our communications network since I had spent a full day with him and had failed to help him level with me.

One of the most common problems in an organization is the process of leveling with third parties instead of one's supervisor. A person may indicate to his supervisor that all is well but communicate complaints and grievances to a third party. In this situation, it is obvious that the person is capable of leveling. The question is: Why can't he level with his supervisor? He needs to realize that his practice can be devastating for the movement and that he is running the risk of being a sower of discord among brothers.

Within Christian organizations more friction and trouble have been caused by "end runs" than by almost any other single mistake. An end run is bypassing or going around a supervisor—going over the head of one's own supervisor to the supervisor's supervisor with a complaint or for any aspect of official business. In effect, the supervisor's supervisor becomes the third party, the one the person levels with.

May every supervisor be alert to detect if he is the terminus of an end run, and may he advise the end runner to go back and follow the line of command. Then, if the person is still unsatisfied, he should ask his own supervisor for permission to appeal to the latter's supervisor. If that step fails to satisfy, the person should be encouraged to appeal to the next person in the line and so on until he is either satisfied or has had his convictions heard by the chief executive.

A fourth element of good communication is the *ability to give and receive mature criticism*. Criticism is essential to a team's growth together—in overcoming weaknesses, reinforcing strengths and fitting into roles needed to make the team function. But one of the mysteries about "Christian organizations" is the presence of a minority element which can criticize unmercifully. Although few in number, they cut, thrust and crush in a spirit of bitterness. Sometimes it masquerades behind a position of theological "righteousness" which results in expression of a loveless orthodoxy. This type of person apparently gains inner satisfaction by stabbing leaders in the back.

Much trouble could be avoided if people would follow three simple communication procedures when they criticize. The first is to go directly to the person you are criticizing. The second is to ask questions before making declarations. It is easy to make general or specific statements criticizing a person or an organization. A more difficult but more productive procedure is first to ask questions in an effort to procure additional information so you can make sure you have sufficient evidence on which to base your criticism. Asking questions also gives the one being criticized a chance to explain his position before receiving the critic's conclusion. Included in your questions should be one asking the person if he has considered alternative procedures and policies.

The role of non-verbal communication can be significant at this point. Be sure to examine the silent messages attached to your questions. A verbal or written communication may appear to be technically interrogative, but the essential message that gets through may be one of declaration, of judgment.

Engaging in criticism by first going to the person directly with your questions preserves respect on both sides. It helps protect you against the charge of trying to be a haughty know-it-all, and it helps insure that the person criticized remains calm, not becoming so threatened that he reacts and becomes overly defensive.

But, suppose for some valid reason the one being criticized is not free to divulge the information which the inquirer is seeking. At such a point the problem boils down to a matter of trust. If a man trusts his colleague, he will return to his post on the battle line and continue to fight against the enemy, not against his fellow soldiers.

The third communication procedure to follow when criticizing is to accompany the criticism with remedial suggestions. To blame a person but suggest no remedial measures or possible alternatives is a form of immature criticism.

You will probably find that your most painful moments in Christian service come when you are on the receiving end of declarative criticism from fellow Christians. It can hurt deeply. Brace yourself for it; ask God to give you a tender heart, an open mind, a strong will—and a thick skin.

hindrances to good communication

Part of the problem in poor communication is that people tend to hear what they want to hear. Each of us is bent toward *selective hearing.* When ill will exists between two parties, they tend to hear from one another that which substantiates their distrust. They tend to put the worst interpretation on what is said and done. On the other hand, where good will exists, the two parties give each other the benefit of the doubt and construe statements to mean what will perpetuate their mutual confidence.

One of the mysteries in communication is how two people, on occasion, can discuss ideas and conclude that they are in agreement but go their ways reporting entirely different stories of what they had agreed on. Some time ago, two friends of mine were experiencing difficulty in working together. When I asked a mutual friend for an explanation, he answered, "It's a conundrum to me. I've been with those two men, heard them conversing, using the same words, agreeing on the same decisions. A week later I've talked with each separately and lo and behold if I didn't get entirely different versions of what they had said and what the decisions were."

To guard against inadvertent selective hearing, it is wise if two or more discussants write down together points on which they are agreeing or disagreeing so that all involved can inspect the phraseology and concur with the statements. One need have his fingers burned only once to realize the importance of getting decisions down into written form. No harm is done if the parties involved each inscribe their initials to the statement, or if carbons are run off so that each carries a copy with him.

Another reason for selective hearing is a person's frame of reference. When intricate policy questions or procedural problems are being discussed, it is possible for a leader to assume that his interrogators are familiar with the existing policies and procedures and to answer them in those frames of reference. If his assumption is valid, his spoken comments will probably be interpreted correctly. But if his listeners have not done their homework or are unfamiliar with the written concepts, they may infer ideas totally different from what he is attempting to communicate. Trouble usually develops subsequently when those listeners observe, "But he said . . . ."

A second hindrance to communication within an organization is *cumbersome and ineffective red tape.* The smaller the organization, the more it can rely on oral communication. Small movements need little in the way of written managerial communication. However, large organizations need more written communiqués. If they have too little, the movement will tend to fragment. It they have too many letters and memoranda, however, they may grind to a halt, ensnared in red tape. Skill is required to achieve the best balance between the oral and written media.

A third hindrance to good communication is the *turnover* in an organization. It takes time, often a long time, to build confidence and neutralize distrust to get a team functioning and communicating properly. A vital link in the communication channels is broken when a person leaves; likewise it takes time to fasten a new link in well when a new person comes.

Newcomers to a movement usually encounter some policies which they think should be changed and some procedures which, in their judgment, should be amended. If you are with IVCF, please rest assured that we want you to think creatively about possible changes in the movement. If you are a new member of a local chapter or a newly appointed campus staff member, your chapter president or your area director and the rest of us will do our best to listen with open minds to your suggestions.

But something else needs to be understood. One of the laws of personal interaction is that suggestions carry more weight if they come from a person who has earned the right to be heard. This takes time and involves two different processes. One is the performance of good works, a record of deeds well done. The other is the asking of good questions which enable one to learn the complexities of issues before he formulates comment.

If you are new to your position, it would be wise to take time to communicate with the people under you, asking: What should I be sure to do in my new position? What should I be careful not to do? What other suggestions do you have for me to consider? By doing this, you will maximize the attention which your suggestions will command by first earning the right to be heard.

A problem related to turnover is *absence.* If you are sick, away on vacation or for some other reason absent from an important session, you would do well to indicate in advance to your team who is going to represent you. A communication failure at this point can confuse your team and set the stage for friction between two or more of them if emergencies arise calling for decisions in your absence. This procedure is especially important if you are a supervisor or a director of a camp or conference.

internal and external communication

Internal communication takes place between two or more members of the team. This is the kind of communication we have been referring to in the previous sections. One tool to help with internal communication is what is called *goal-support grid*. It is the sharing between colleagues of thoughts on how "you" could help "me" perform my job better and how "I" could help "you" perform your job better.

If the spirit of a team is healthy, this sharing, this internal communication can be brief; it need not be elaborate. Speed-memos and postcards can serve in lieu of letters, phrases instead of clauses.

However, essential to maintaining this kind of communication are longer and regular *reports*. Reports are a type of communication in which a team member describes or analyzes progress and problems for someone entitled to such information and in which he gives account of the responsibility and authority entrusted to him. A healthy management team reports promptly and adequately.

Reporting may seem like a burden at times. If so, it will help to remember the reasons for having written reports: First, written reports can be tools enabling a person to take stock of himself and compare his progress with his goals. For this reason alone, the writing of a report should be profitable even if no one else ever reads it. In this connection, the reporting format should follow a person's goals and standards. Also, written reports keep a person's supervisor informed so that he can do a better job of helping the person. And those reports enable the supervisor to report more effectively to his supervisor. Lastly, adequate reporting is one way of communicating to a person's supervisor that he respects him and deems him worthy of the time and energy required to provide the information to which he is entitled. In this respect internal reports can strengthen the spirit of fellowship in a team.

Some report formats include a question or more dealing with morale in general and grievances in particular. If communication is to be healthy within a movement, it is essential that people be honest in their reporting, especially when they express grievances. Failure to level in a written report but then leveling in oral dialog with someone other than a person's supervisor is devastating for both that person and the organization as a whole, as we have said.

When the communication network reveals internal discontent, it does no good to "sweep things under the rug," ignoring the problem. Leaders should ask the Lord for wisdom and then procure a clear picture of symptoms of the discontent, the specific complaints. Then a leader should endeavor to understand the causes behind the complaints and, finally, to attempt to work out remedial solutions to alleviate the grievances.

Many of these considerations apply to external communication as well. External communication takes place between a member of the team and others outside the team. There are two extremes to avoid: undercommunication whereby we fail to answer correspondence or to provide adequate information, and overcommunication whereby we inundate the recipient with more ideas and information than is desirable.

The three major linkages of IVCF staff are with the board which employs us, with the campus groups we serve and with the public which supports us. We must determine the necessary balance between oral and written reports in external communication so that good relations can be promoted and maintained.

A special problem in external communication occurs when you work closely with a person employed by another organization and problems develop between you. If you disapprove of something the person is doing or have questions which imply disapproval with his sphere of influence, never discuss these with his supervisor until you have discussed them with the person in question—and given him time (with the benefit of your counsel) to work out a solution. If he fails to respond to this approach the first time, contact him again. Do not call or confer with his supervisor until he has had ample opportunity to handle the problem.

If you write the person a letter disapproving of something in his sphere, never send a carbon to his supervisor. The person may interpret this as an indication that you feel he is not really in control of the situation or that you are using the occasion to impress his boss with your own wisdom and rightness. Sending such a carbon will strike a body blow to whatever confidence the person has in you.

Similarly with letters to his supervisor, never write complaints about the particular person (even with a carbon to go to him) until you have contacted him and given him time to explain the problem and work out a remedy. If you insist on going over his head, you are likely to insult him.

practical considerations for leaders

In the process of organizing, a manager is bound to come upon the problem of how many people one man should be responsible to and responsible for. Generally, a person in one position should be responsible to only one person. The stage is set for confusion if he is responsible to two or more. However, it is possible for one person to split his attention among two or more positions. He should then have a separate job description for each position, and in each position he should be responsible to only one supervisor.

The ideal number of people one man can be responsible for varies with the type of organization, types of jobs and types of people. The term *span of responsibility* or *span of control* is used to connote the number of people who report directly to one supervisor. If all one's supervisees have similar job descriptions, he can supervise more persons than if they have different job descriptions. The upper limit for any leader is the number he can be directly responsible for without being spread too thin.

If you are a group leader, you may on occasion have a member causing trouble for reasons you can share with few other people. This is a touchy problem. The person may be kind, patient, considerate, courteous, gentle and gracious in his relationships with his supervisees and peers. People love him. But, privately, with you his supervisor, he is brusque, impatient, opposite to the traits which recommend him to other people. Invariably, this type of person will differ with you on at least a few decisions. The opinion difference may become known. If his supervisees and other friends side with him and are either perplexed by your intransigence or antagonistic toward you, you will have to navigate rough waters. There isn't much to do except pray that God will give you wisdom and power to do the right thing—and then remain true to that guidance in spite of the unpleasant relationships and criticism from other parties.

checkpoints for leaders

Have you double-checked to make sure that each person who reports directly to you has a clear picture in his mind of his areas of responsibility—to whom? for whom? for what?—and that his answers are in writing? Do you know that the people who report to you have made sure that the people who report to them (and on down the line) have equally clear and correct answers to those three questions in writing? Beware of taking this for granted. It is easy to assume that everyone is clear and in agreement, but your job is to make sure there is no uncertainty.

More specifically, does each person on your team have a written job description? Is he satisfied with it? Have copies been circulated (or at least posted in a public place) among all people under his supervision? A tinder box for trouble is set if a leader lets even one of his people work without a written job description or if he fails to see that copies are distributed to the appropriate people.

Have you checked to make sure that an organization chart has been constructed showing the relationships between all people under your supervision, that this chart is on display in a location where all your people can see it, that all of your people have inspected it and have a clear picture of where they fit into it and that they have been requested by their supervisors to point out any errors they see in the chart? It is not enough to "think" that all of your people know what the chart "looks like."

Are you maintaining a spirit of loyalty on your team and are you alert to signs of disloyalty? Do you encourage your team and commend them privately on a job well done? Mark Twain once said, "I can live for at least a month on one good compliment."

Are you doing everything possible to keep the communication channels in your organization wide open, both verbally and non-verbally? Are you creating a climate which helps everyone level with their appropriate supervisors and supervisees? Are you making sure that decisions get put down in writing so that possible misunderstanding can be prevented?

If we want our colleagues to feel like members of one team, one of the indicators that our communications are healthy will be the tendency for our people to use the pronouns *we, our* and *us* instead of *you, your, they* and *them* when referring to the organization. A danger signal may be flying when a colleague uses the plural *you* and *they* instead of *we* and *us*.

recapitulation

In any organization, there is continued tension within a person between his responsibilities to his leaders and his yearning to enjoy the fruits of freedom. This tension can be compounded in a Christian organization if a person begins to conclude that his responsibilities to his human leaders are interfering with his obligations to the Lord.

However, if one's leaders are men of God, and if one is convinced that the Lord Jesus has called him to serve in that organization, then he can with expectation and joy follow the admonitions in Scripture:

Remember your leaders, those who spoke to you the word of God; consider the outcome of their life, and imitate their faith. (Heb. 13:7)

Obey your leaders and submit to them; for they are keeping watch over your souls, as men who will have to give account. (Heb. 13:17)

Let us commit our total persons to the Holy Spirit; let us then under his control organize our work so as to discharge our time, energy and use of donor gifts as good stewards of the potential which God has given us.

4 review

Review comes during and after the action of planning and execution. During review we pause to observe our deeds and compare the results with our objectives, goals and standards. Review should include evaluation.

One of the major motivating forces in a movement is the interest leaders express in what their people are doing. Lower echelons in the team are stimulated to do what their leaders *inspect,* not what they expect. The average person has no idea what his supervisor thinks of him unless he hears from the boss himself; he is smart enough to know that he isn't perfect and he expects his boss to be smart enough to help him do better.

the importance of goals and standards in review
When a man sits down to review his performance with his supervisor, the discussion may be of little benefit, if not a waste of time, unless goals and standards have been written down and mutually accepted in advance. Without such standards the

review session is likely to be characterized by a reluctance to face issues, failure to level with each other for fear of hurting feelings, evaluations based on subjective opinions (which may differ sharply between the two parties) and unrecognized differences of opinion as to whether the performance of either has been satisfactory.

One of the most unpleasant experiences in a team occurs when a supervisor decides that a subordinate must be released because of unsatisfactory performance—and the subordinate is caught by surprise. Such an incident is painful for both parties and can seriously shake the morale of others on the team. Such experiences can be prevented by the use of good standards in review sessions. Properly employed, good standards will signal the subordinate far in advance that his release is probable if he does not improve. This reason alone should motivate a person to construct standards mutually acceptable to himself and his supervisor.

On the other hand, with the use of standards, a review session can be fruitful, quickly identifying those areas in which the individual can derive satisfaction from a job well done and pinpointing those areas in which he needs help. Such a review maximizes the time in which a supervisor can help his supervisee where he needs assistance. (Appendix D gives an example of how goals and standards can be designed for use in a review session.)

private and corporate review

Review must be conducted on two levels: review of an individual and review of a group or team.

There are four dimensions to review of an individual. The first is review alone, privately comparing your performance with your goals and standards. Ideally, your written reports should be a fruit of such private review. After a person has reviewed himself, he then is reviewed by people who know him—his supervisor, his supervisees and his peers. These three reviews should ideally be handled in separate review conferences.

A group or team should also collectively review its performance. The group should construct its own goals and standards and have these approved by its leader. There is within any organization the intelligence, experience and ability to discover what is wrong with operations and to plan ways and means to correct those conditions—provided management gives the members of the group both the time and the means to express themselves in this way.

scheduling a review conference

The responsibility for scheduling and leading review conferences should be borne by the supervisor. Supervisees feel more secure if they see that their supervisor cares enough about them to take time to sit down privately in unhurried fashion and go step by step through goals and standards. On the other hand, every supervisee should feel that he always has the privilege of requesting a review conference—in the event that his supervisor forgets. But, unless the supervisor accepts his responsibility, there is little likelihood that profitable review conferences will be held anywhere in the team he is supposed to lead.

Accordingly, it is wise procedure for the supervisor to construct an entry in his goals and standards dealing with review conferences which he will conduct privately with each supervisee and corporately with the team he leads. The supervisee should also construct an entry in his goals and standards dealing with review conferences which he intends to participate in with his supervisor.

Some supervisors, new to their responsibilities, may feel a bit awkward in attempting to schedule review conferences. If so, a simple written note to the supervisee might suffice, such as "Could we get together sometime in the next two weeks for a couple hours of review conference?"

conducting a review conference

A healthy review conference is one in which both parties discuss each other's work with the view to being mutually helpful. It is not a glad-handing or back-patting party. Nor is it a grilling inquisition to be feared by either. Rather, it is a two-way street whereby you ask the other person for help in evaluating your work in terms of your plans (that is, your objectives, goals and standards) and you offer your help in evaluating the other person's work in terms of his plans. Helpful questions are: What am I doing well? (What is he doing well?) Where do I need help? (Where does he need help?) What can be done to help me? (What can be done to help him?) What is my potential for the future? (What is his potential for the future?) A review session is incomplete unless both parties speak the truth with love to one another as to whether they think the other is doing a satisfactory job and unless both offer tangible suggestions as to how the other can improve.

Opening a review conference may sometimes be difficult. In such instances it may be helpful for the supervisor to open the conversation with leading questions such as: What is your biggest headache? What is your most enjoyable blessing? What is your thorniest problem? How do you feel? The purpose of the leading question is to help set a climate in which a person can open up if he desires.

One of the most difficult things to accomplish in a review conference is the venting of dissatisfaction. Yet this is one of the most important targets which a conference should hit. If a supervisee is dissatisfied, his supervisor must know about it so that together they can resolve the problem.

To air dissatisfaction in a healthy fashion, two specific people must take two specific steps. First, the supervisor should structure the formats for both written reports and the agenda for personal interviews or conferences to include a specific, explicit statement by the supervisee as to whether he is satisfied with the supervision he is receiving and with the way other things are going in the movement. A supervisor is defaulting on an obligation if he fails to ask a supervisee explicitly, from time to time, if he is satisfied with the supervision.

Second, the supervisee should respond in all honesty to these opportunities in both his written reports and his review conferences. Standards are incomplete if they contain no entry concerning an evaluation of the supervision one is receiving. A supervisee is defaulting on a trust if he disapproves of his supervision but goes through a review with his supervisor and fails to direct the supervisor's attention to the dissatisfaction.

As a result of the airing of dissatisfaction or other feelings, a review conference may indicate that a change should be made somewhere in a man's performance. Helpful questions can be: What do you think I should do that I am not doing? What do you think I should stop doing? What do you think I should continue—but do differently?

the outcome of review

If problems have existed within a team, a properly conducted review conference will have exposed them. Now it is up to the team to work together and solve the surfaced problems.

One of the most serious of these problems is overload of a person. Overload produces stress and anxiety which are contagious and can devastate team morale. If a person is frustrated over an extended time by "too much to be done," the explanation generally can be found in one or more of the following conditions:

First, he may not be managing his work properly. He either may not have the load strapped properly to his shoulders or not know how to carry it. If this is the problem, he should apply the principles spelled out in this book.

Second, the load itself may be too large for him no matter how well he straps it on or attempts to manage it. The demands may exceed his potentialities or at least call for different services than his endowments enable him to provide. It may be that he has reached his "level of incompetence."

Third, the team to which he belongs may be so poorly managed that it is hard for him to carry on his work.

When a person is overworked—feeling crushed by the load and experiencing excessive stress and strain—who is to blame? The primary fault lies with the overloaded person's immediate supervisor. He should be the first to observe the overload problem and to take remedial steps to bring the load back to bearable size. The fault also lies with the supervisor's supervisor (and with all intermediate supervisors up to and including the chief executive officer). If these people are managing their work properly, they should have some sort of alarm system which signals whenever and wherever overload occurs in the movement. Finally, the overloaded person himself is to blame for failing to manage his work properly or to mention the problem as soon as it began to build up.

recapitulation

The importance of goals and standards to review (whether private or corporate) cannot be overemphasized. Indeed, the best agenda for a private review period or a review conference is a man's goals and standards. Every set of standards should contain an entry concerning the frequency of the person's private review sessions, review conferences with his supervisor and review conferences with each supervisee.

Trouble brews when a person thinks he is doing well but his leader evaluates him as doing poorly. The best solution is the use of standards which are drawn up, written down and approved in advance by both a man and his leader. If standards are properly constructed—and circulated—all these people should be able to agree on whether a person is doing a good job: himself, his supervisor, his peers and his team.

5   how to proceed

Before constructing your objectives, goals and standards, pause to reflect on the following ideas and to study the indicated documents. Although the following paragraphs are cast in terms of an IVCF field staff member, they can be applied with only slight modification to an IVCF chapter president, a cell group leader, pastor, board chairman and so forth.

how to proceed as an individual
Remember that, as an IVCF staff member, you are a minister. God assigns his people to different ministries and helps prepare them by giving them different gifts. Each IVCF member is therefore unique; yet he is part of a whole, a movement which is unified by its purposes, basis of faith and organization.

Study the following: the Articles of Incorporation, the by-laws, the operational procedures, our policy manual, *One Team,* the job description of your president and the job descriptions of the other supervisors between you and the president.

Review your own job description, if you already have one, and either reaffirm your committal or revise it with the approval of your supervisor. If you do not have one in written form, immediately construct a job description. Take it to your supervisor for approval and then distribute copies of the approved description to him and to each person whom you supervise.

Review *Training in IVCF.* Remember that your number one service is training the people for whom you are responsible. This document gives a host of suggestions as to how you can be a more effective trainer.

Study the conditions that now exist in your sphere of responsibility and the available resources (including your time, talents and reservoir of energy).

Go to Scripture as you commence to construct your own objectives, goals and standards. Expect that the Holy Spirit will use the Bible in guiding you as you lay out your plans.

Except the Lord build the house, those who build it labor in vain. (Ps. 127:1)

For we are his workmanship, created in Christ Jesus for good works, which God prepared beforehand, that we should walk in them. (Eph. 2:10)

Pray. Ask the Lord to guide your mind as you formulate your plans.

For I know the plans I have for you, says the Lord, plans for welfare and not for evil, to give you a future and a hope. (Jer. 29:11)

Construct your objectives. In order that your plans be congruent with your responsibilities, it is generally best to take each major entry in your job description and let it stand as an objective. Often you can take those entries verbatim for use as objectives. Then construct goals and standards under each objective. Set standards high enough to be a challenge yet not so high as to frustrate you when you fall short.

Remember that one of the differences between a goal and a standard is objectivity. A statement is a goal if different people might hold different opinions as to whether or not you have reached it; it is a standard if all evaluators reach the same verdict concerning your performance relative to it.

Draw up your goals and standards for the year. There should be two types of entries insofar as the calendar is concerned: those which commit you for specific dates (sketch on a worksheet such as our "Year-at-a-Glance" or a "Seven Star Diary," etc.) and those which involve no specific dates (construct a "Yearly Totem Pole of Priorities").

Draw up your goals and standards for next month. Again there should be two types of entries: Construct a "Month-at-a-Glance" and also a "Monthly Totem Pole of Priorities."

Draw up goals and standards for today. A 3 x 5 card should be sufficient for including both scheduled events and priorities.

Unless you express your plans via the calendar (or some other "budgetary expression of time") your plans are likely to remain in the realm of theory rather than practicality.

Take the initiative in discussing your objectives, goals and standards with your supervisor. Procure his approval.

Provide your supervisor with a copy of your goals and standards. If you fail to do this, he is likely to wonder what the reasons are for your failure to make such provision. Also give a copy of your goals and standards to each of your peers and to each person you supervise—so that they can get a clearer picture of the job they are supposed to be helping you accomplish.

Read *Tyranny of the Urgent* (IVP, 25¢) as preparation for execution and review.

Execute your plans as expressed in your goals and standards.

Review. First, review privately. Set some sort of schedule you wish to follow in conducting your private reviews; for example, once a month. Then review with your supervisor. Prior to each review conference it might be helpful to recall the ideas presented in chapter four. It is wise to set some sort of schedule for these, too; for example, once every six months.

how to proceed as a group leader

If you are a group leader (regional director, area director, department head, president of a local IVCF chapter, leader of a cell group, chairman of a local committee, pastor, etc.), you have another lap to go, this time as the leader of a group in planning, executing and reviewing its work. Adapt for yourself the following suggestions (sculptured in terms of an IVCF staff member):

Gather your group together. You may wish to include only those who report to you directly. Begin by reiterating the concept that you are all members of the same body, ministering to each other by using your individual God-given gifts.

Double-check to see that each person is committed to the basis of faith and purposes and that he is gladly abiding by the policy manual (after careful study, not simple scanning). Emphasize the basic premises undergirding our movement.

Discuss with them once a year as a group first the president's objectives, goals and standards and then your own. The purpose here is not to show off how ambitious the president is or how impressive you are. Rather, there are at least three reasons they should possess and understand these plans and understand the contents: First, they are entitled to know how you and I view our jobs and how we are going about the task of getting them done. Second, we need their help. It is impossible for us to hit our goals and to reach our standards without their collaboration. They are essential compatriots in our venture and without them you and I will fail. We want them to have as clear a picture as possible of those duties in which we need their assistance. And last, copies of our goals and standards may serve as useful examples to them as they go about the task of formulating their own objectives, goals and standards.

Review with them *Managing Our Work* and *Training in IVCF.* Study as a group some selected Scripture passages for guiding the team in group planning. Pray together seeking God's will—his plans for your team.

Together, go through the annual plan and the long-range plan for IVCF as a national movement. Both these plans should "brew from below" and all your team should have opportunity to contribute to their construction. In any case, study both plans with your group, each member of which should possess a personal copy. Ask them for any changes they care to suggest. Forward these to your supervisor.

Collectively sketch out in rough form an annual plan and a long-range plan for your group. Insofar as possible, organize the ideas around the same format as used for the national plans. Because each cabinet member is expected to provide copies of his team's annual and long-range plans to the other cabinet members and each area director is expected to provide copies of his group's plans to his regional director and to other area directors in his region, it will be easier all around if these plans follow the same general format.

As a planning aid, it might help to post a large map of the territory served by your team. (If yours is a metropolitan area you might wish to refer to the Army Map Service edition at a scale of approximately 1:60,000). Plot the location of such variables as schools with affiliated IVCF chapters, schools with unaffiliated groups, schools with informal contacts, strategic schools with no contact as yet, churches which are with us, residences of staff, associate staff and other resource people and other locations significant in your planning.

Express the plans in objectives, goals and standards for the group as a whole.

Based on those plans, draw up the group's goals and standards for next month or next semester, whatever your interval is.

Discuss the group's plans with your supervisor. Procure his approval. Produce a finished draft. Provide copies to your team, peers and supervisor. Remember that if a plan is to qualify as "good," it must be constructed in terms of objectives, goals and standards based on factual evaluations of the past and present, constructed with involvement by the supervisees, assigned in terms of tasks and times and a useful tool for progress.

Check to make sure that each member is satisfied with his

own job description. Explain how his job description fits into your objectives and goals; that is, how he helps you get your job done.

Help each team member construct objectives, goals and standards for himself as an individual. He must understand the rationale of this and have studied *Managing Our Work*.

Suppose that one of your supervisees fails to provide you with an acceptable copy of his goals and standards. What might you do? Sometime when he is in a relaxed mood, ask him if he has read *Managing Our Work* and if he agrees with the ideas in it. If he answers No, your job is to try to convince him of the potential value of goals and standards. If he answers Yes, your job is to help him take that first step in constructing goals and standards.

You might indicate that you know from experience how difficult such construction is and then ask something like, "What seems to be the obstacle preventing your coming up with my copy of your goals and standards?" Be prepared for almost anything at this point. As you discern what the hang-up is, you can offer remedial suggestions. Assure him that at this stage of the game a rough draft is acceptable. Ask him to set a deadline (request that he drop you a note of this in writing) acceptable to both of you as to when the rough draft will be in your hand. If he misses that deadline, you might say something as follows, "I know how hard it is to set goals onto paper. Would you be offended if I took your job description and sketched out some thought-starter objectives, goals and standards in order to help you get started?" He may be greatly relieved to have you offer such assistance. But if he resists at this point, something is wrong somewhere. Only close probing to help him level with you can reveal where the trouble lies.

From time to time, visit each team member on his job. Work with him shoulder to shoulder, using his plan as the guideline.

Conduct team meetings regularly. The purposes of a team meeting are to help the members be more Christlike in character and do as good a job as possible with the responsibilities spelled out in their job descriptions. The frequency of these meetings will depend on how you and your team work. There need to be enough meetings to foster a spirit of cohesiveness and to provide opportunities for training, to hammer out plans and procedures, to share information and ideas and to get better acquainted. On the other hand, if staff meetings are held too often, they drain away time and energy from other essential work. The IVCF cabinet meets five or six times a year. An area team should meet probably once a month or so. A camp staff team should meet at least once a week during camping season.

The less the geographic distance between team members, the more frequent can be the team meetings without straining the transportation budget. Teams widely scattered may need some sort of subsidy for transportation if they are to benefit from frequent staff meetings.

A manager's check list is given in Appendix E. It may help you to evaluate your growth as a manager.

6 management for growth

Good management enables a man to be a better steward of the time and talents God has given him. We manage our work by planning objectives, goals, standards, programs and procedures. Then, we execute those plans and review the results. In light of the review, we revise our objectives, goals, standards, programs and procedures and then return to action to carry out these revisions, confident that "God is at work in you, both to will and to work for his good pleasure" (Phil. 2:13). Our plans may be superb from man's viewpoint, but unless the Holy Spirit is energizing us as we spell out such plans and as we work to fulfill them, we will accomplish nothing. Let us look to the Lord Jesus (Heb. 12:2) and "have regard for him who planned it long ago" (Is. 22:11).

Looking back over the management process as a whole, it is wise to remember that our movement will grow only as its people grow, not primarily in number but in quality. If people are not growing, the fault lies basically with us who lead.

the presuppositions of a good manager

People are more likely to grow if their leaders build on the following assumptions. Each person has a built-in drive toward growth and self-realization. An interest in working effectively, the potential for development, the capacity for assuming responsibility, the readiness to work toward the attainment of goals—all are present in all our people. They will work toward the achievement of a movement's objectives and goals to the degree that they are committed to those purposes, objectives and goals. And they will become committed to objectives and goals to the degree that they have become involved in formulating them and in measuring their own performance, as well as in controlling their own surroundings.

Prompt, candid, meaningful feedback from a man on his performance is necessary for him to experience a feeling of achievement. Where there is disagreement in this feedback, a leader must remember that a person's behavior is justifiable to himself and is based on how he sees himself and his surroundings. A leader must try to put himself in the person's place.

And, finally, a leader will presuppose that his people want his help. People feel secure when the leadership is both firm and fair.

characteristics of effective management

The higher one moves in the management team, the greater should be the percentage of his time and effort spent in planning and review and the less in execution. This is a difficult lesson for most people to learn.

A good manager knows, too, that the higher he goes in the management pyramid, the greater will be his realization that someone somewhere is always disgruntled about something. On the other hand, there is usually someone somewhere who is pleased with the way things are going. But a manager is on the road to ruin if he lets his popularity become a factor in his decision making. To be sure, every manager desires that his people think that their organization is good and that he is a good leader—but it is essential that his popularity (if any) be earned with the right people and for the right reasons. Otherwise his popularity may ruin the morale he desires to build.

Given these basic mind-sets of a manager, his management will be effective if it is further characterized by the following: (1) participation by his people at all levels in the determination of objectives, goals and standards for themselves as individuals and for their team as a group; (2) placement of decision making and problem solving at the lowest level it can be done effectively and with full accountability; and (3) performance, in the most effective way possible, of only that work which will make a definite, recognizable contribution toward attaining the objectives of the team.

To insure these characteristics, a leader will regularly discuss with each team leader to clearly delineate and define what each one's area of responsibility is, what he is to do, what authority he has to carry it out, what rules he must follow and what results will be acceptable. If he is leading well, he will emphasize results more than methods and give more attention to what is done, rather than how. He will leave the methods up to the individual to work out.

This will require that he make it plain to every member that each person has the freedom to make mistakes and have them viewed as part of the learning process. The climate thus created will be an open and problem-solving one where disagreement is handled without fear so that there is an atmosphere of mutual trust and confidence throughout the movement.

appendix a

example of a job description of a board of trustees

board of trustees of Inter-Varsity Christian Fellowship

1. Sets the course of IVCF as a movement. Formulates major policy and long-range plans.
2. Reserves selected powers of decision-making.
3. Delegates all other powers.
4. Elects the chief executive officer.
5. Approves appointment of staff who report directly to the chief executive.
6. Provides advice, counsel and assistance to the management.
7. Approves the budget.
8. Approves major capital expenditure.
9. Reviews the progress of the movement and takes appropriate action.
10. Creates adequate machinery for fulfilling board responsibilities including perpetuation of a healthy board.
11. Identifies the board's needs for information from management.

appendix b

example of a job description of a board member

board member of Inter-Varsity Christian Fellowship

1. Lives a life in which the fruits of the Holy Spirit are evident.
2. Is a member of a local church or assembly. Participates regularly in Christian fellowship.
3. Attends the meetings of the board.
4. Gives financially in proportion to his ability, demonstrating unusually strong interest in Inter-Varsity.
5. Signs each year our statement of agreement with the IVCF purposes and basis of faith.
6. Participates in various phases of Inter-Varsity's ministry, such as:
a. Prays regularly for IVCF, probably using Intercessor.
b. Serves as a member of a local committee, or faculty advisor, or associate staff member or active member of some other supportive group.
c. Reads HIS and IVP publications.
d. Entertains IVCF staff members.
e. Arranges as appropriate for an annual presentation of IVCF in his home church.
f. Informs friends and others about IVCF.
7. Participates jointly with other trustees in carrying out the responsibilities listed in the job description for the board as a corporate whole.
8. Accepts appointment to board committees.
9. Performs the study and homework prerequisite for board meetings and committee meetings.
10. Acquires a broad knowledge of IVCF.
11. Provides advice and counsel to management but refrains from involving himself in management.
12. Identifies situations in which he has special competence or contacts and makes these known to the board and to the president.

appendix c

example of a job description of a chief executive

the president of IVCF

frame of reference

Inter-Varsity believes that God is at work at institutions of higher learning, calling out a people for his name. The Holy Spirit has not bypassed the college campus; he is operating there as elsewhere in both the salvation of unbelievers and the strengthening of believers, making them increasingly conformable to the image of our Lord Jesus Christ.

God uses many instruments as he pursues his work on the campus. One of these is Inter-Varsity Christian Fellowship. Every IVCF staff member, regardless of position, is expected to operate under the authority of God communicated to him through the Holy Spirit in harmony with the Bible. Moreover we believe that God's Spirit has called the leaders of IVCF to their positions and that, through their past experience and present supply of information, they are to be instruments in his hands to train and direct staff members under them.

IVCF as a national movement is to be a channel through which every staff member is provided with considerable prayer support, encouragement, salary, literature, training and direction.

Every staff member is to be in agreement with IVCF's doctrinal basis and statement of purposes and to abide by our policies and procedures as spelled out in the Policy Manual. He is expected to be a man of God and to do those deeds which will glorify God not only through IVCF but in every aspect of his life.

Within such a frame of reference every staff member is expected to shoulder responsibilities within two broad categories: (1) personal development and family relationships, and (2) service, responsibilities of his particular position.

personal development and family relationships

He is a maturing disciple of Jesus Christ.
He develops his intellectual potential.

He endeavors to maintain physical and emotional health.
If married, he is the faithful head of a Christian home.
He participates in Christian fellowship.

service

The president is the chief executive officer and, as authorized by the
board of trustees, is responsible for the total work of Inter-Varsity
Christian Fellowship in maintaining its doctrinal integrity and fulfilling
its purposes. Within the limits of the articles of incorporation,
by-laws and operational procedures, the president is responsible for
and has the commensurate authority to perform the services
set forth below.

1. Recruits, appoints, directs, trains, encourages and gives leadership by
precept and example to the staff in both field and headquarters in
order to fulfill IVCF's purposes of evangelism, discipleship and missions.
Fosters within the movement a healthy climate and vibrant esprit de
corps which stimulates each person to function at his best.
Formulates policies, plans, objectives, goals, standards, programs and
procedures for the staff, including Nurses Christian Fellowship
and Foreign Missions Fellowship.
2. Raises the total financial support.
3. Maintains budgetary control, accounting all income and controlling
all expenditures.
4. Keeps abreast of current world conditions, especially those in
the college world in order to fulfill IVCF's ministry in it.
5. Directs publication of literature which will assist IVCF personnel to
fulfill their purposes.
6. Safeguards and maintains all physical assets.

representation

1. Serves as chief representative of IVCF with the public and as liaison
representative with the International Fellowship of Evangelical Students.
2. Directs publication of all material designed to inform the public
about IVCF.

reports

1. Provides the board with adequate reports. Informs the board about
conditions within IVCF. Invites board counsel. Recommends board
approval for major policy proposals. Sees that board study
committees are properly informed.
2. Supervises a system of reporting within the staff.

appendix d

goals and standards for use in review sessions—taken
from those of the president of IVCF

	In my opinion the president's performance relative to the indicated goals and standards:		
	is falling short.	is reaching.	is surpassing.
objective a: To recruit, appoint, direct, train, encourage and give leadership by precept and example to the staff in both field and headquarters in order to fulfill IVCF's purposes of evangelism, discipleship and missions; to foster within the movement a healthy climate and vibrant esprit de corps which stimulates each person to function at his best; to formulate policies, plans, objectives, goals, standards, programs and procedures for the staff including Nurses Christian Fellowship and Foreign Missions Fellowship.			
goal 1 As a maturing disciple of Christ to maintain a godly life which will be an example of Christ-centered living. "Men are looking for better methods; God is looking for better men." Character comes first.			
goal 2 Ever to keep before the movement the principle that quality comes before quantity and that both are important.	___	___	___
goal 3 To see that communication lines are open for suggestions of revisions to our policies, strategies, programs and procedures from staff, board, local committees, students, faculty and any other person with helpful comments about IVCF and our ministry.	___	___	___
goal 4 To lead in formulating and conducting a strong training program.	___	___	___
standard 4.1 The president responds within ten days to each report from a cabinet member.	___	___	___

standard 4.2 Cabinet meetings are held five times a year.

standard 4.3 The president visits each region twice a year to assist the regional director in his ministry and to learn from him. Preferably one of these visits is to coincide with a regional staff conference.

standard 4.4 On each major field trip the president meets with (a) one student executive committee and (b) one student chapter for training and feedback purposes.

appendix e

manager's check list

	yes	no	not sure
1/Do you have a written job description indicating to whom, for what, and for whom you are responsible?	—	—	—
2/Are you managing your work according to a written set of objectives, goals and standards (OGS)?	—	—	—

you and your supervisor

	yes	no	not sure
3/Have you provided him with a copy of your OGS?	—	—	—
4/Has he approved them?	—	—	—
5/Has he provided you with a set of his OGS so that you might see how your work fits into a larger picture?	—	—	—
6/Do you report to him at least once a month (or more frequently at his request) and receive acknowledgement as to the adequacy of each report?	—	—	—
7/Do you have at least two unhurried review sessions (of the type described in Managing Our Work) per year with him?	—	—	—

you and your "cabinet"

	yes	no	not sure
8/Does each of your supervisees have a written job description?	—	—	—
9/Have you provided a set of your OGS to each of your supervisees and discussed them so that he understands what he is expected to help you accomplish?			

10/Is each of your supervisees managing his work
according to OGS which you have approved?

___ ___ ___

11/Does each report to you at least once a month?

___ ___ ___

12/Do you acknowledge each report, indicating its
adequacy and responding in an effort to be of help?

___ ___ ___

13/Do you conduct a satisfactory number of
"cabinet" meetings in which all your supervisees
assemble as a group to plan and review their
work—as individuals and as a team?

___ ___ ___

14/Have you gone through Managing Our Work
with them?

___ ___ ___

15/Does your "cabinet" (that is, those who report
directly to you) have a written annual plan
spelled out in terms of objectives, goals and standards
for the "cabinet" as a whole?

___ ___ ___

16/Do you conduct at least two unhurried
review sessions per year with each of your supervisees according to the review principles
in Managing Our Work?

___ ___ ___

the rest of your team

17/Have you posted or circulated an organization
chart showing the position of every person
under your jurisdiction?

___ ___ ___

18/Does every such person have a written
job description?

___ ___ ___

19/Is each managing his work according to a
written set of OGS?

___ ___ ___

20/Has each supervisor provided a copy of his OGS
to each of his supervisees?

___ ___ ___

21/Does each supervisee report at least monthly
to his supervisor?

___ ___ ___

22/Does each supervisor conduct an unhurried
review at least semi-annually with each of
his supervisees?

_____   ____ ____ ____

23/Does each supervisor conduct satisfactory staff
meetings of his team as a whole?

_____   ____ ____ ____

24/Has each supervisor led his team in
constructing an annual plan for the team as
a whole?

_____   ____ ____ ____

25/Does your entire team understand who is
in authority when you are absent?

_____   ____ ____ ____

26/Does each supervisor make clear who is in
charge of his team when he is absent?

_____   ____ ____ ____

bibliography

general management

Allen, Louis A. *The Management Profession.* McGraw-Hill, 1964.

Black, James M. *Developing Competent Subordinates.* American Management Assn., 1961.

Bower, Marvin. *The Will to Manage.* McGraw-Hill, 1966.

Clowney, Edmund P. "Resource of Divine Guidance: The Bible and Management Principles," unpublished mimeographed document, undated. Available from Westminster Theological Seminary, Philadelphia, Pennsylvania.

Dayton, Edward R. *God's Purpose/Man's Plans.* Missions Advanced Research and Communications Center, 1971.

Drucker, Peter F. *The Practice of Management.* Harper and Row, 1954.

———. *The Effective Executive.* Harper and Row, 1966.

Engstrom, Ted W. and Alec MacKenzie. *Managing Your Time.* Zondervan, 1967.

Ewing, David W., ed. *Long-Range Planning for Management.* Harper and Row, 1964.

Ford, George L. *Management for Christian Workers.* Zondervan, 1964.

Ford, Guy B. *Building a Winning Employee Team.* American Management Assn., 1964.

Kahn, Robert L. and Elise Boulding. *Power and Conflict in Organizations.* Basic Books, Inc., 1964.

Killian, Ray A. *Managing by Design.* American Management Assn., 1968.

Morgan, John S. *Improving Your Creativity on the Job.* American Management Assn., 1968.

Steiner, George A., ed. *Managerial Long-Range Planning,* McGraw-Hill, 1963.

Urwick, L. *Elements of Administration.* Pitman and Sons, 1947.

planning

Graves, Clare W. "Deterioration of Work Standards." *Harvard Business Review,* September-October, 1966, pp. 117-126.

Hughes, Charles L. *Goal Setting.* American Management Assn., 1965.

McCay, James T. *The Management of Time.* Prentice-Hall, 1959.

Odiorne, George S. *Management Decisions by Objectives.* Prentice-Hall, 1969.

Osborn, Alex F. *Applied Imagination.* Scribners, 1956.

organization

Dale, Ernest. *Organization.* American Management Assn., 1967.

motivation

Gardner, John W. *Self-Renewal.* Harper and Row, 1963.

Gelberman, Saul W. *Management by Motivation.* American Management Assn., 1968.

Meyers, Scott. *Every Employee a Manager.* McGraw-Hill, 1970.

Prime, Derek. *A Christian's Guide to Leadership.* Hodder and Stoughton, 1964.

Russell, G. Hugh and Kenneth Black. *Human Behavior and Life Insurance.* Prentice-Hall, 1963.

Schoonmaker, Alan N. *Anxiety and the Executive.* American Management Assn., 1969.

Wilson, James I. *The Principles of War.* Continental Press, 1964.

training

Osborn, Alex. *Wake Up Your Mind.* Scribners, 1952.

communication

Haney, William V. *Communication and Organizational Behavior.* Richard D. Irwin, Inc., 1967.

review

Kellogg, Marion S. *What to Do About Performance Appraisal.* American Management Assn., 1965.